4 W's + 1

Effective Marketing for Contractors

MY CONTRACTOR ASSIST

MyContractorAssist.com

Table of Contents

Introduction 1
   Our Approach: A Case Study 7
Chapter 2: The 4 W's 9
   The What...11
   The Who..13
   The When...15
   The Where..18
   Practical Application: A Seasonal Strategy 21
Chapter 3: The How   Implementing the 4 W's.....24
   DIY vs. Professional Assistance............................24
   Easy-to-Use Software 24
     Case Study: Simplified Social Media Campaign...24
Chapter 4: Managing Leads Effectively................25
Chapter 5: The Plus 1 30
Chapter 6: Conclusion 34

MyContractorAssist.com

Introduction

Welcome to My Contractor Assist, a comprehensive solution designed to address the challenges faced by contractors in today's demanding business environment. Understanding that contractors often feel overwhelmed, overworked, and underpaid, caught in an endless cycle of seeking new clients, quoting jobs, and hiring staff, we have developed a unique program that can help you grow your business, save money, and increase your bottom line.

With over 20 years of experience in construction and contracting, we have worked with a diverse clientele, including residential, commercial, municipal, and industrial sectors. Our team of experts has a deep understanding of the challenges and opportunities faced by contractors and is dedicated to providing innovative solutions that can make a real difference in your business.

This micro book is just a glimpse into the wealth of knowledge and expertise offered by My Contractor Assist. Through this book, we will focus on one of our processes to demonstrate how we can either save you money through efficient cost management strategies or help you market your business effectively to reach new clients and increase your ROI.

MyContractorAssist.com

We believe in showing you our capabilities rather than simply convincing you of our expertise. By providing tangible examples and case studies, we will illustrate how our program can help you overcome common pain points and achieve sustainable growth.

Visit our website at www.mycontractorassist.com to learn more about our comprehensive program and how it can benefit your contracting business. Let us partner with you to unlock your full potential and help you achieve success in the competitive world of contracting.

Visit www.mycontractorassist.com

MyContractorAssist.com

Chapter 1: Traditional Advertising

Have you tried a marketing company before?

In today's competitive digital landscape, partnering with a marketing company seems like a no-brainer. After all, they promise a wealth of expertise, resources, and connections to help businesses reach new heights. However, many companies, like ours, have embarked on this journey only to be met with disappointment.

We've tried several marketing companies and website designers and found very similar results: lots of promises but no significant ROI.

Despite investing thousands of dollars monthly into their services and ad campaigns, the results were far from satisfactory. Leads generated were of poor quality, and conversions were minimal. It's as though our marketing efforts were swallowed up by a black hole, leaving us with little to show for it.

After spending thousands of dollars monthly on their services and ad campaigns, we ended up with poor-quality leads and minimal conversions.

The frustration was palpable. We couldn't understand why, despite our significant financial commitment, the promised results remained elusive. It seemed as if our marketing partners were more interested in securing our business than in delivering tangible outcomes.

MyContractorAssist.com

At least we got some impressive but expensive websites out of it.

Amidst the disappointment, there was one consolation: the websites created by these companies were visually stunning. While aesthetics are important, they alone cannot drive business growth. A website is only as effective as its ability to attract, engage, and convert visitors into customers.

We knew there was a better way, there just had to be.

We refused to accept mediocrity. We believed there was a better way, a marketing approach that would deliver real, measurable results. Fueled by this conviction, we embarked on a quest to find a true marketing partner who understood our goals and was committed to our success.

Common Challenges with Traditional Marketing

Project Value Mismatch

Our initial challenge was the project value. We were focused on residential clients, requiring a minimum project value of $10,000 to cover our costs and profit margin, aiming for projects over $40,000. Despite clearly communicating this to the marketing company, we consistently received leads for projects significantly below the $10,000 threshold. For example, over a four-month period, we spent $5,000 monthly on marketing services, excluding ad costs for Facebook and Google ads. However, this investment resulted in only two

MyContractorAssist.com

potential clients—one with a budget of $5,000 for a $20,000 project and another with a budget mismatch for a $40,000 project. Unfortunately, neither lead had the financial resources to complete their respective projects. Consequently, the return on our $31,893.31 investment was $0.

Poor Lead Quality

In addition to the project value mismatch, we also encountered poor lead quality from our marketing campaigns. Over a three-month period, we spent approximately $12,000 on a combination of Facebook and Google ads, generating over 497,000 impressions. However, none of these impressions resulted in substantial leads. The ads targeted a broad audience, leading to wasted ad spend on unqualified prospects who were not interested in our services.

Misaligned Vision

Another significant challenge was the difficulty in communicating our vision to marketing agencies. Many of the agencies we worked with lacked a deep understanding of the contracting industry, which resulted in ineffective campaigns. For instance, they would create ads targeting homeowners for landscaping services in densely commercial areas where there was limited potential for residential projects. This misalignment led to wasted marketing efforts and poor lead generation results.

MyContractorAssist.com

Ownership and Control Issues

Furthermore, we faced ownership and control issues with some marketing agencies. Many agencies insisted on hosting our website on their platforms, making it difficult and expensive for us to retain ownership of our digital presence if the relationship ended. This led to situations where we had to rebuild our website multiple times, which was time-consuming and costly. The lack of control over our website also limited our ability to make changes and updates efficiently.

MyContractorAssist.com

Our Approach: A Case Study

Our campaign's primary objective was to assess the reach and targeting effectiveness of a particular client profile. To achieve this, we implemented a two-week Facebook ad campaign with a modest budget of $257.53. Our efforts yielded 7,120 impressions, offering valuable insights into the platform's reach and targeting capabilities.

In contrast, we concurrently conducted a Google ad campaign, where we invested $449.99. This strategic decision enabled us to gather crucial data on Google's reach and targeting potential. Our Google campaign generated an impressive 102,745 impressions, significantly surpassing our Facebook campaign's reach.

The pivotal distinction between our approach and traditional marketing agencies lies in our ability to target a specific market segment. By narrowing our target market to the top 40% income bracket, we strategically focused our resources on individuals with a higher propensity to convert into paying customers. This targeted strategy allowed us to achieve better results with a fraction of the budget typically spent by traditional agencies on broad, untargeted campaigns.

One of the key takeaways from this experiment is the importance of avoiding unnecessary ad spend on unqualified leads. By precisely targeting a well-defined audience, we maximized our return on investment (ROI) and avoided the pitfalls associated with broad

MyContractorAssist.com

targeting. Our approach allowed us to allocate our budget more efficiently, ensuring that our ads were seen by individuals who were genuinely interested in our offerings.

In conclusion, our Facebook and Google ad campaigns provided valuable insights into the reach and targeting capabilities of both platforms. By leveraging targeted marketing strategies, we were able to achieve significant results with a limited budget, outperforming traditional agencies' broad targeting approaches. This successful experiment underscores the importance of tailoring marketing campaigns to specific audiences, enabling businesses to optimize their ROI and reach their desired target market effectively.

MyContractorAssist.com

Chapter 2: The 4 W's

Marketing your business can indeed seem like an overwhelming task, but by breaking it down into four key elements—What, Who, When, and Where—you can make it much more manageable.

- **What**:
    - Clearly define the products or services you offer.
    - Determine the unique selling points and benefits of your business.
    - Understand your value proposition and how it sets you apart from competitors.
- **Who**:
    - Identify your target audience and understand their needs, wants, and pain points.
    - Research demographics, psychographics, and behaviors to create detailed customer personas.
    - Segment your audience into groups based on common interests and characteristics.
- **When**:
    - Determine the best time to reach your audience with your marketing messages.
    - Consider factors such as industry trends, seasonal patterns, and holidays.
    - Plan your marketing campaigns to align with key events and opportunities.

MyContractorAssist.com

- **Where**
  - Choose the right marketing channels to reach your target audience effectively.
  - This may include online platforms like social media, search engines, email marketing, and e-commerce websites.
  - Consider traditional channels such as print advertising, television, and radio.

MyContractorAssist.com

The What

When it comes to explaining your product or service, particularly in industries like contracting, effectively communicating its value and unique features can be a challenge. While you, as a business owner, have a deep understanding of your offerings, conveying that knowledge to an external audience, especially those unfamiliar with the industry, requires careful consideration.

Advertising professionals, often experienced in consumer products and services, may not fully grasp the nuances of contracting. This can lead to marketing materials that fail to accurately represent your services and the value you provide. To ensure your marketing efforts resonate with your target audience, it's crucial to take the time to craft clear and compelling messaging that communicates your product or service's benefits.

Start by breaking down your product or service into its core components. Identify the specific elements that make your offering unique and valuable. What are the problems your product or service solves? What are the benefits customers can expect to experience? Once you have a clear understanding of these elements, you can start to develop messaging that speaks directly to your target audience's needs and desires.

Use language that is accessible and easy to understand. Avoid industry jargon or technical terms that may alienate or confuse your audience. Instead,

MyContractorAssist.com

focus on using simple, everyday language that clearly explains the benefits of your product or service.

Incorporate storytelling into your marketing materials. Share real-life examples of how your product or service has helped customers achieve their goals. These stories can help potential customers connect with your brand on a personal level and see how your offering can positively impact their lives.

Highlight your value proposition. What sets your product or service apart from the competition? What unique benefits do you offer? Make sure your marketing materials clearly articulate your value proposition and why customers should choose you over others. Use strong visuals to support your messaging. Images and videos can help to bring your product or service to life and make it more tangible for potential customers. Choose high-quality visuals that are relevant to your target audience and that align with your brand identity.

By taking the time to develop clear, compelling messaging and utilizing effective marketing strategies, you can ensure that your marketing materials accurately reflect your services and the value you provide. This will help you to attract new customers, build brand awareness, and drive growth for your contracting business.

MyContractorAssist.com

The Who

Understanding your target audience is a critical aspect of developing effective marketing strategies. Different groups of potential clients have unique needs, preferences, and decision-making processes, so it's essential to tailor your marketing efforts accordingly.

Residential Homeowners

Residential homeowners are often focused on improving their living spaces and increasing the value of their properties. They may be interested in home improvement projects such as kitchen renovations, bathroom upgrades, landscaping, and energy-efficient solutions. When marketing to residential homeowners, it's important to emphasize the benefits of enhanced comfort, convenience, and aesthetics. Visuals, testimonials, and case studies can be effective in showcasing the transformation that your products or services can bring to their homes.

Commercial Property Managers

Commercial property managers are responsible for maintaining and optimizing commercial spaces such as office buildings, retail centers, and industrial facilities. Their primary concerns include cost-effectiveness, durability, and tenant satisfaction. When targeting commercial property managers, highlight the long-term value and return on investment of your products or services. Emphasize how your solutions can help them

MyContractorAssist.com

reduce operating costs, improve energy efficiency, and attract and retain tenants.

Municipal Decision-Makers

Municipal decision-makers, such as city council members, mayors, and public works officials, are responsible for making decisions that impact the community's infrastructure and public spaces. They are often focused on sustainability, safety, and community well-being. When marketing to municipal decision-makers, it's essential to demonstrate how your products or services can contribute to the betterment of the community. Highlight their potential to enhance public safety, reduce environmental impact, and improve the quality of life for residents.

Understanding the distinct characteristics of each target group allows you to tailor your marketing messages, channels, and strategies to resonate with their specific needs and priorities. It's not just about the price point; it's about understanding the decision-making criteria and motivations that drive their purchasing behavior. By focusing on the unique value proposition for each group, you can create marketing campaigns that are relevant, compelling, and more likely to drive conversions.

MyContractorAssist.com

The When

Timing is of paramount importance when it comes to marketing your services in the contracting industry. By aligning your marketing efforts with seasonal demand, you can significantly increase your chances of success and achieve a higher return on investment (ROI).

Consider the following strategies:

1. Snow Removal Services:
    - Target Audience: Homeowners, businesses, and property management companies.
    - Best Time to Market: Mid to late summer to early fall.
    - Messaging: Emphasize the importance of being prepared for winter weather and the benefits of early booking. Offer special discounts and promotions to incentivize early sign-ups.
2. Roofing Services:
    - Target Audience: Homeowners, businesses, and commercial property owners.
    - Best Time to Market: Late winter to early spring.
    - Messaging: Highlight the importance of roof maintenance and repairs before the rainy season begins. Offer free inspections and consultations to assess roof conditions and recommend necessary services.

MyContractorAssist.com

3. Landscaping Services:
   - Target Audience: Homeowners, businesses, and municipalities.
   - Best Time to Market: Late winter to early spring.
   - Messaging: Promote spring clean-up services, lawn care packages, and landscape design consultations. Offer discounts on bundled services to encourage comprehensive lawn care solutions.
4. Home Improvement Services:
   - Target Audience: Homeowners and property investors.
   - Best Time to Market: Spring and summer.
   - Messaging: Focus on home improvement projects that enhance curb appeal and increase property value. Offer financing options and highlight the benefits of energy-efficient upgrades.
5. Pest Control Services:
   - Target Audience: Homeowners, businesses, and property managers.
   - Best Time to Market: Early Spring to summer.
   - Messaging: Emphasize the importance of preventative pest control measures to protect properties from infestations. Offer seasonal pest control packages tailored to specific pest problems.

MyContractorAssist.com

Remember, the key is to understand your target audience's needs and align your marketing efforts accordingly. By leveraging seasonal demand, you can capture the attention of prospective customers and position your services as the solution to their needs.

MyContractorAssist.com

The Where

Geographic targeting is a fundamental aspect of marketing that requires careful consideration. It involves identifying specific geographic locations where marketing efforts should be focused to reach the target audience effectively. By doing so, businesses can optimize their resources and achieve better results. Here's why geographic targeting is essential and how it can impact your marketing strategy:

1. Reaching the Right Audience:
   Geographic targeting allows you to pinpoint the areas where your target customers are located. This ensures that your marketing messages reach the people who are most likely to be interested in your products or services. For example, if you're a local restaurant, it makes sense to focus your marketing efforts on the neighborhoods or towns surrounding your establishment rather than targeting a broader region.

2. Efficient Use of Resources:
   By focusing on specific geographic areas, you can allocate your marketing budget more efficiently. Instead of spreading your resources thin across a large region, you can concentrate on the areas that have the highest potential for generating leads and sales. This helps you avoid wasting time, money, and effort on marketing to people who are unlikely to become customers.

MyContractorAssist.com

3. Tailored Marketing Messages:
Geographic targeting enables you to tailor your marketing messages to the specific needs and preferences of your target audience in different locations. By understanding the local demographics, cultural influences, and consumer behavior, you can create marketing campaigns that resonate with the people you're trying to reach. For instance, if you're targeting a coastal region, you might highlight the proximity of your beachside resort in your marketing materials.

4. Competitive Advantage:
Geographic targeting can provide you with a competitive advantage by allowing you to focus on underserved markets or areas where your competitors have a weaker presence. By identifying these opportunities, you can position your business as the go-to choice for customers in those areas and gain a foothold in new markets.

5. Measurable Results:
Geographic targeting makes it easier to track the results of your marketing efforts. By monitoring key metrics such as website traffic, leads generated, and sales closed in specific locations, you can assess the effectiveness of your campaigns and make data-driven decisions to optimize your strategy.

Overall, geographic targeting is a vital component of any successful marketing strategy. By focusing your efforts on the right geographic areas, you can reach the

MyContractorAssist.com

right audience, use your resources efficiently, tailor your marketing messages, gain a competitive advantage, and measure your results effectively.

MyContractorAssist.com

Practical Application: A Seasonal Strategy

Landscaping businesses can significantly boost their success by implementing a seasonal marketing strategy that aligns with the changing needs of their clients throughout the year. Here's how:

Early Spring (Late Winter):

- **Spring Cleanup and Lawn Care Services:** As the first signs of spring emerge, homeowners are eager to shake off the winter blues and bring their yards back to life. Capitalize on this enthusiasm by promoting spring cleanup services, such as removing leaves and debris, aerating lawns, and trimming shrubs.
- **Lawn Care Packages:** Offer special packages that combine multiple services, such as mowing, fertilizing, and weed control, at a discounted rate. This encourages customers to invest in comprehensive lawn care and ensures a steady stream of revenue for your business.

MyContractorAssist.com

Mid-Spring to Early Summer:

- **Garden Design and Outdoor Living Spaces:**
  As the weather warms up, people start thinking about spending more time outdoors. Promote design services to help clients create beautiful outdoor spaces. Offer consultations, design plans, and installation services to cater to different needs and budgets.
- **Outdoor Living Products:**
  Partner with suppliers to offer outdoor furniture, grills, fire pits, and other accessories. This allows you to provide a one-stop-shop for customers looking to enhance their outdoor living areas.

Late Summer to Early Fall:

- **Leaf Removal and Winter Preparation Services:**
  As the leaves start to fall, homeowners face the daunting task of leaf removal. Promote leaf removal services, including cleanup, bagging, and disposal. Offer discounts for early booking to encourage customers to secure their spots before the rush.
- **Winter Preparation Services:**
  Educate clients on the importance of preparing their landscapes for winter. Offer services such as mulching, pruning, and winterizing irrigation systems to protect plants and ensure a healthy start in the spring.

MyContractorAssist.com

Year-Round Services:

- **Ongoing Maintenance:**
  Offer year-round maintenance services, such as regular mowing, weeding, and pest control, to ensure that your clients' landscapes stay looking their best throughout the year.
- **Seasonal Consultations:**
  Provide seasonal consultations to assess clients' needs and recommend appropriate services. This proactive approach helps build trust and loyalty, as clients appreciate your commitment to their satisfaction.
- **Customer Loyalty Programs:**
  Implement customer loyalty programs that reward repeat customers with discounts, free services, or early access to promotions. This encourages customers to stay with your business and helps you retain a steady client base.

By aligning your marketing efforts with the seasons, you can ensure that your landscaping business is top-of-mind for clients when they need your services the most. This strategic approach not only maximizes your revenue but also fosters long-term relationships with your customers.

MyContractorAssist.com

Chapter 3: The How Implementing the 4 W's

You might be wondering how to implement the 4 W's. Here's where our systems come in.

DIY vs. Professional Assistance

Through MyContractorAssist.com, you have options. You can access and train on our software and tools to handle your marketing, we can manage it for you, or you can choose a hybrid model. The choice is yours.

Easy-to-Use Software

Our software is designed to be user-friendly, requiring no programming or development skills. We offer quick setup options, whether you have a current website or not. Our tools help you develop funnels, landing pages, websites, and ads, making it easy to manage your marketing efforts.

Case Study: Simplified Social Media Campaign

One of our clients, a roofing contractor, used our software to create a social media campaign targeting homeowners in high-income neighborhoods. By utilizing our templates and tools, they set up the campaign within a few hours. The result was a 30% increase in leads and a significant boost in ROI compared to their previous traditional marketing efforts.

MyContractorAssist.com

Chapter 4: Managing Leads Effectively

Once your ads are live, managing leads efficiently is crucial.

Centralized Lead Management: Unifying Platforms and Optimizing Communication

Our software revolutionizes lead management by consolidating all leads from various platforms into a single, centralized hub. This eliminates the risk of missed opportunities and streamlines communication with potential customers.

Our groundbreaking software redefines lead management by offering an innovative approach that consolidates leads from diverse platforms into a unified, centralized hub. This revolutionary system eliminates the risk of missed opportunities, empowering businesses to capture every potential connection.

With our advanced technology, all leads from various sources, such as websites, social media, email campaigns, and more, are seamlessly integrated into a single, comprehensive platform. This consolidation ensures that no lead falls through the cracks, allowing businesses to maintain a comprehensive view of their entire lead pool.

By centralizing lead information, our software streamlines communication with potential customers.

MyContractorAssist.com

All interactions, including emails, text messages and notes, are automatically recorded and linked to the respective lead profiles. This enables sales teams to access a complete history of customer interactions, ensuring that every conversation is informed and personalized.

Moreover, our intuitive platform provides real-time updates on lead status and engagement levels. With this valuable insight, businesses can prioritize their efforts, focusing on the most promising leads and nurturing relationships. This data-driven approach empowers sales teams to make informed decisions, optimize their strategies, and improve their conversion rates.

Furthermore, our software offers robust analytics capabilities, enabling businesses to analyze lead sources, track performance metrics, and identify areas for improvement. These insights help organizations optimize their lead generation efforts, allocate resources effectively, and maximize their return on investment.

By revolutionizing lead management, our software empowers businesses to connect with potential customers more efficiently and effectively. With a centralized hub, streamlined communication, real-time insights, and advanced analytics, our platform equips sales teams with the tools they need to succeed in today's competitive market.

MyContractorAssist.com

Key Features of Our Centralized Lead Management System:

1. Consolidated Lead Capture:

- Integrates with multiple platforms such as Google, Facebook, your website, text messages, and phone calls.
- Captures leads from all these sources and centralizes them in one place.
- Provides a unified view of all leads, making it easy to manage and track.

2. Real-Time Lead Distribution:

- Distributes leads evenly among sales representatives or teams.
- Ensures fair and equitable distribution of leads based on predefined criteria.
- Eliminates the need for manual lead assignment, saving time and effort.

3. Streamlined Communication:

- Enables quick and efficient communication with leads through various channels.
- Allows sales representatives to respond to leads promptly, increasing the chances of conversion.
- Tracks all interactions with leads, providing a comprehensive record of communication.

MyContractorAssist.com

4. CRM Integration:

- Seamlessly integrates with your existing CRM system.
- Automatically logs all lead interactions and communication within the CRM.
- Provides a holistic view of customer relationships, from initial contact to project completion.

5. Automated Lead Nurturing:

- Triggers automated email campaigns and marketing messages based on lead behavior.
- Nurtures leads through personalized content and offers, increasing engagement and conversion rates.
- Saves time and resources by automating the lead nurturing process.

MyContractorAssist.com

Real-Life Example: Increased Sales for an E-commerce Business

An e-commerce company implemented our centralized lead management system and experienced a significant increase in sales. By having all leads in one place, sales representatives were able to respond quickly and effectively, leading to higher conversion rates. The automated lead nurturing feature also played a crucial role in engaging leads and moving them through the sales funnel.

MyContractorAssist.com

Chapter 5: The Plus 1

Before we talk about The Plus 1 we want to give you something to consider: The Power of Language in Marketing

Consider the words you use in advertising.

Which is more appealing:

"Discount" or "Affordable"?

The answer depends on your desired outcome. "Discount" implies reduced prices, which might attract bargain hunters but could undervalue your service. "Affordable," on the other hand, suggests value without compromising quality, appealing to clients who appreciate both cost and quality.

In today's competitive marketing landscape, mastering the fundamental 4 W's - What, Where, Why, and Who - is essential. However, there's an additional element that can elevate your campaigns to new heights - the Plus 1. This enigmatic factor, often overlooked yet profoundly impactful, holds the key to unlocking the ultimate goal: WINNING.

The Plus 1 represents the essence of effective lead management. When you meticulously execute the 4 W's and manage your leads with precision, the fifth element, WINNING, becomes a natural consequence. Marketing campaigns strive for success, and WINNING

MyContractorAssist.com

embodies the pinnacle of achievement. At My Contract Assist, we have several processes to assist you with "Closing the Deal" aka WINNING.

To harness the power of the Plus 1, several techniques can be employed. One crucial strategy involves establishing a clear and compelling value proposition. By articulating the unique benefits and advantages your product or service offers, you create a compelling reason for potential customers to choose you over your competitors. Additionally, personalizing your marketing messages to resonate with individual customer needs and preferences can significantly increase engagement and conversions.

Another effective technique is to leverage social proof. Testimonials, reviews, and case studies from satisfied customers add credibility and trustworthiness to your brand.

These positive endorsements from real people can significantly influence hesitant buyers and nudge them closer to making a purchase.

Furthermore, creating a sense of urgency through limited-time offers or exclusive promotions can motivate customers to act promptly. By instilling a fear of missing out, you increase the likelihood of immediate sales.

MyContractorAssist.com

Nurturing leads through automated email marketing campaigns plays a pivotal role in enhancing customer engagement and fostering loyalty. This strategic approach involves delivering personalized, relevant, and valuable content to leads at different stages of the sales funnel. By leveraging automation, businesses can streamline their lead nurturing efforts, ensuring that each lead receives the right message at the right time.

At the core of this process lies the creation of automated email sequences that cater to the unique needs and interests of each lead segment. These sequences can encompass a wide range of messages, including welcome emails, educational pieces, product recommendations, case studies, and promotional offers. By providing valuable insights, addressing customer concerns, and offering tailored recommendations, businesses can gradually build trust and credibility with leads.

My Contractor Assist has mastered the automation process for lead management with a few tweaks that would customize the process to fit your business needs. Personalization is key to successful lead nurturing campaigns. By leveraging data and analytics, businesses can segment their leads based on various criteria, such as demographics, behavior, and engagement history. This segmentation allows for the delivery of highly targeted email messages that resonate with each lead's individual needs and preferences. Personalized subject lines, body copy,

MyContractorAssist.com

and images can significantly increase open rates and click-through rates, driving leads further down the sales funnel.

Automation also enables businesses to track and measure the effectiveness of their lead nurturing campaigns. Detailed reports and analytics provide insights into key metrics such as open rates, click-through rates, conversions, and revenue generated. This data-driven approach allows businesses to optimize their campaigns continuously, refining their strategies and improving results over time.

By nurturing leads through automated email marketing campaigns, businesses can create a seamless and personalized customer experience that fosters long-term engagement and loyalty. This approach not only helps convert leads into paying customers but also builds a strong foundation for ongoing relationships, increasing customer lifetime value and overall business growth.

Remember, WINNING is not merely an outcome but a mindset. It's about continuously striving for excellence, refining your strategies, and adapting to the ever-changing marketing landscape. By embracing the Plus 1 and incorporating these techniques into your campaigns, you can unlock the full potential of your marketing efforts and consistently achieve the desired results. So, go forth and conquer the marketing world with the power of the Plus 1!

MyContractorAssist.com

Chapter 6: Conclusion

Our mission, as we mentioned at the outset, was to share practical insights into how we optimized our procedures to reduce advertising expenses and increase ROI. However, our knowledge extends far beyond what we've already shared. We have a treasure trove of cost-saving advice and methods that we're eager to impart to you.

You've probably experienced the frustration of seeing your advertising costs spiral out of control while your return on investment (ROI) stagnates. If so, you're not alone. Many businesses struggle with this exact problem. But what if we told you there was a way to turn things around?

That's exactly what we've done at My Contractor Assist. Through a combination of strategic planning, data analysis, and creative problem-solving, we've managed to lower our advertising costs and increase our ROI significantly. And we're not just talking about a marginal improvement—we're talking about a major transformation.

So, how did we do it? We're glad you asked. Here are some of the key strategies that we employed:

1. **We conducted a comprehensive audit of our advertising campaigns.** This helped us identify areas where we were spending too much money and not getting enough results.

MyContractorAssist.com

2. **We implemented a data-driven approach to advertising.** We used analytics to track the performance of our campaigns and make adjustments as needed.

3. **We focused on creating high-quality, engaging content.** We knew that if we could create content that our audience would love, they would be more likely to click on our ads and convert into customers.

4. **We experimented with different advertising platforms and tactics.** We didn't just stick to the same old methods—we were willing to try new things to see what worked best.

5. **We partnered with a team of experts.** We knew that we couldn't do this alone, so we brought in a team of experienced professionals who could help us develop and implement our strategies.

The results of our efforts have been nothing short of remarkable. We've seen a significant decrease in our advertising costs and a substantial increase in our ROI. And we're not just talking about a short-term improvement—we're talking about a long-term transformation.

We know that not every business is the same, so what worked for us may not work for you. But we believe that

MyContractorAssist.com

the principles we used can be applied to any business that wants to improve its advertising results.

If you're ready to take your advertising to the next level, we encourage you to reach out to us at www.mycontractorassist.com. We'll be happy to help you develop a customized plan that's tailored to your specific needs.

MyContractorAssist.com

www.ingramcontent.com/pod-product-compliance
Lightning Source LLC
Chambersburg PA
CBHW072056230526
45479CB00010B/1096